How Did They Do That?

Lisa Klobuchar

sundance™

sundance™

Copyright © 2005   Sundance/Newbridge, LLC

All rights reserved. No part of this publication may be reproduced or transmitted in any form or by any means, electronic or mechanical, including photocopy, recording, or any information or retrieval system, without permission in writing from the publisher.

Published by
Sundance Publishing, LLC
33 Boston Post Road West
Suite 440
Marlborough, MA 01752
800-343-8204
www.sundancepub.com

How Did They Do That?
ISBN 978-0-7608-9633-4

Illustrations by Kevin Rechin; pp. 11 (top) and 18 (bottom) by Jim Kopp

Photo Credits:
Cover (pyramids) ©Charles & Josette Lenars/CORBIS, (rocket) NASA;
p. 1 NASA; p. 6 ©Aladin Abdel Naby/Reuters/CORBIS; pp. 6–7 ©Royalty-Free/CORBIS; p. 7 ©Carl & Ann Purcell/CORBIS; p. 8 ©Bettmann/CORBIS;
p. 9 Brand X Pictures/FotoSearch; p. 10 ©Nik Wheeler/CORBIS; pp. 10–11 ©Bettmann/CORBIS; p. 11 ©Archivo Iconografico, S.A./CORBIS; p. 14 (top) ©George Hoeylaerts, (bottom) ©CORBIS; p. 16 ©CORBIS; p. 17 (top) ©George Hoeylaerts, (bottom) ©Bettmann/CORBIS; p. 19 ©CORBIS; p. 20 (top) ©CORBIS, (bottom) ©Jeff Greenberg/Index Stock Imagery, Inc.;
p. 21 ©Yogi, Inc./CORBIS; pp. 24–26 NASA; p. 27 (top) NASA, (bottom) photo by Neil A. Armstrong/NASA; pp. 28–29 NASA

Printed in China

10/09-225542

Table of Contents

The Pyramids of Giza

Imagine standing in the shadow of one of the towering stone Pyramids of Giza on the west bank of the Nile River in Egypt. You stare up in amazement wondering how people could possibly have built it over 4,000 years ago.

The Pyramids of Giza—one of the Seven Wonders of the Ancient World—were built to stand forever. Each of the three largest was a royal tomb for an Egyptian king. The pyramids held everything the Egyptians thought a king's spirit would need to make his travels to life after death an easy one. Treasures of gold, furniture, even food were buried with the king.

Some mysteries about these massive stone mountains may never be fully solved. But let's find out why they were built and who built them, and explore a theory about how they were built.

Who Built the Pyramids?

Think about a baseball stadium full of people. Now think about trying to organize all 20,000 to 30,000 people to build one gigantic pyramid!

Workers for the Pharaoh

Ancient Egyptians believed their **pharaoh**, or king, was the son of a god. They thought that after he died he became part of Osiris, the king of the dead. They felt his body needed protection so that his soul could continue to live forever. The Egyptians believed the pharaoh could continue to take care of Egypt in his afterlife. So he was **mummified** and then buried in his pyramid.

A 2,500-year-old mummy and coffin were discovered in a tomb near the step pyramid of Sakkara.

Some of the pyramid workers were skilled. Others were farmers and **peasants** whom the pharaoh's men ordered to work during the three to four months every year when the Nile River flooded. Most of the farm workers probably worked willingly. This is because they believed their pharaoh's influence with the gods kept the Nile flooding each year. And that allowed them to grow their crops.

The Great Pyramid was once about 481 feet tall. It is now about 450 feet tall without its smooth outer layer.

Who Did What?

The thousands of skilled workers included architects, stonecutters, metalworkers, and masons. They were sent to work and live at the building site or at the quarries where the stone was dug. The villages where they lived were supervised by the pharaoh's men. These workers built the pyramids without any of the cranes, jackhammers, or modern technology we have today. Knowing this makes it even more amazing that the giant structures exist at all!

WHERE DID THE TREASURES GO?

In the burial chamber of the dead king, and sometimes in other chambers of a pyramid, there were many treasures, including gold and precious jewelry. The builders tried to make the pyramids thief-proof by hiding entrances and sealing off internal passageways with heavy stones after the king's burial. But robbers somehow broke into the pyramids and stole most of the riches.

Skulls and debris in a looted tomb

7

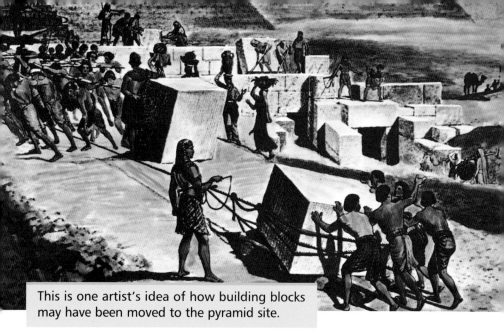

This is one artist's idea of how building blocks may have been moved to the pyramid site.

The thousands of farmers and unskilled workers did the physical labor of pulling and dragging the huge stone blocks of the pyramids into place. They worked in groups that may have even competed with each other. They used more than two million blocks to build the largest of the Pyramids of Giza. Sometimes it took as many as twenty men to drag one block. That's because each block weighed about 2-1/2 tons or about the same weight as 25 refrigerators!

One pyramid block weighs as much as 25 refrigerators.

Staggering Stone Skyscrapers

Think about how much area ten football fields would cover. This is the size of the base of ONE pyramid!

First: The Perfect Position

Building a pyramid in just the right position was very important. It had to be built so the king's soul would have the most direct route to the gods. The base of the pyramid is a perfect square, and the sides face exactly north, south, east, and west. But how did the ancient Egyptians make such accurate measurements?

An **astronomer**-priest observed the stars to find which direction was true north. From this point, his assistants measured the four corners of the site and marked out a perfect square. Then the building could begin.

The Nile River

One Layer at a Time

We don't know exactly how the pyramids were built, but we know that they were constructed by adding one layer of stone blocks on top of another. We also know that the measurement of these layers had to be exact. If they were wrong, a small error at the bottom would have thrown everything off.

450 feet

Great Pyramid of Giza

THAT IS BIG!

For over 4,000 years, The Great Pyramid was the tallest building in the world! See how it compares with the height of some of today's structures.

316 feet

305 feet

179 feet

Leaning Tower of Pisa

Statue of Liberty

Big Ben

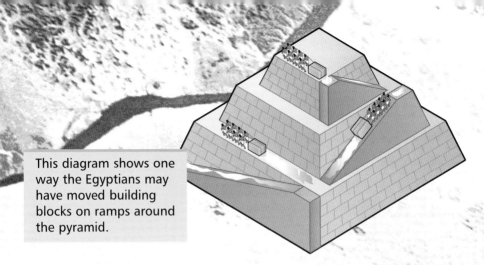

This diagram shows one way the Egyptians may have moved building blocks on ramps around the pyramid.

One theory is that workers built ramps that curved around the outside of the pyramid. Once the huge blocks of stone arrived on boats floated down the Nile River, the blocks were put on **sledges**, or sleds. The workers dragged these sledges up the ramps. The ramps may have had water on them to ease the movement of the sledges. As each layer of the pyramid was finished, the ramps were raised and lengthened. Imagine the size of the ramps needed to build the huge Great Pyramid.

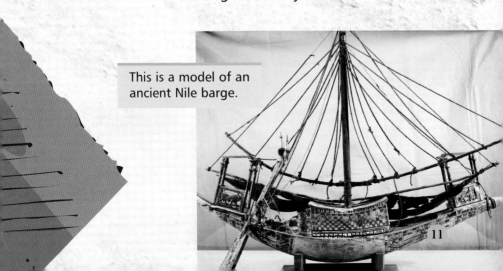

This is a model of an ancient Nile barge.

The Panama Canal

Sea voyages between the Atlantic and Pacific oceans weren't always as easy as paying a toll and cruising about 51 miles along a waterway.

Over 100 years ago, a voyage from the Atlantic Ocean to the Pacific Ocean took many months. If a ship sailed from New York City to San Francisco, it would have to travel around South America. The trip was about 15,000 miles. But today, you can make the same trip by traveling less than half of that distance—about 6,000 miles! This is possible thanks to one of the world's most spectacular engineering achievements—the Panama Canal.

The struggle to build the canal went on for many years. Here is how the story begins. . . .

The French Disaster

For hundreds of years, people had dreamed of ways to connect the Atlantic and Pacific oceans. Finally, the country of France decided to try building a canal in the Central American country of Panama.

No Easy Task

The narrow strip of land in Panama that separated the two oceans by about 50 miles seemed like the logical place to build a canal. So in 1882, French planners hired people to begin digging a canal that would run at sea level across the **isthmus**. They decided to dig straight down into the rock and soil across the swampy jungles of the isthmus. But they soon realized it wasn't that simple!

In 1896, French workers use an excavator to remove rocks and dirt.

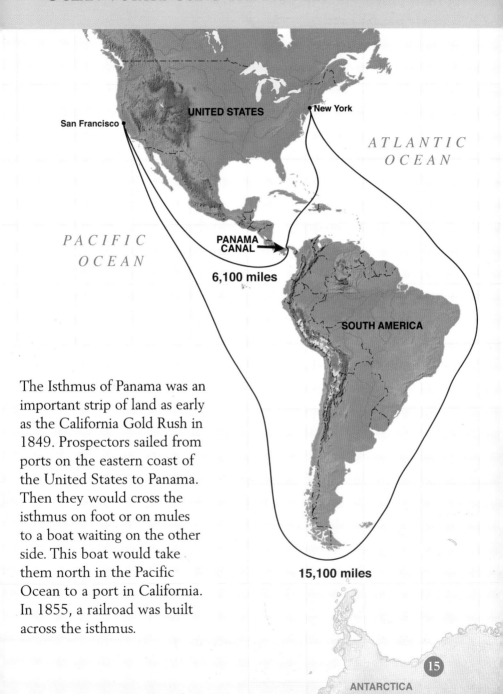

United States

San Francisco

New York

ATLANTIC OCEAN

PACIFIC OCEAN

PANAMA CANAL

6,100 miles

SOUTH AMERICA

15,100 miles

ANTARCTICA

The Isthmus of Panama was an important strip of land as early as the California Gold Rush in 1849. Prospectors sailed from ports on the eastern coast of the United States to Panama. Then they would cross the isthmus on foot or on mules to a boat waiting on the other side. This boat would take them north in the Pacific Ocean to a port in California. In 1855, a railroad was built across the isthmus.

15

Big Problems

It didn't take long for the French to realize they didn't have the proper tools or materials to handle the water or the **landslides** that occurred as they dug. Rocky hills, thick tropical rain forests, deep swamps, blistering heat, heavy rainfalls, and river flooding all made the canal construction difficult and dangerous. And then there were the deadly diseases.

Mysterious Deaths

The steamy heat and tropical conditions in the Isthmus of Panama made it a perfect place for mosquitoes. Many of these carried diseases, like yellow fever and malaria, that were transmitted to people through insect bites. But at the time, the French didn't know this was how people got these diseases. At least 20,000 people had died because of disease by the time the French gave up on the canal project in the late 1890s.

Yellow fever cage

WHAT WAS YELLOW FEVER?

Yellow fever is a virus that is carried by some mosquitoes that live in tropical and jungle areas. The mosquito's bite can send the virus into a person's body, causing the person to contract the disease. A person with yellow fever can have a fever, headaches, sore muscles, and an upset stomach. But the symptom that is most telling is when the skin starts to look yellow due to liver damage. That's how the disease got its name. Today, people who travel to tropical areas get a vaccine that helps prevent the disease.

The Americans Give It a Try

In 1902, the United States Congress gave President Roosevelt permission to proceed with building a canal across the Isthmus of Panama.

Darn you Americans!

Wiping Out the Mosquitoes

In 1904, Dr. William Gorgas of the U.S. Army took charge of cleaning up the canal area and getting rid of the mosquitoes. He had workers drain swamps and clear large areas of brush and grass where the mosquitoes lived. Then they sprayed chemicals to kill the insects. By the end of 1905, yellow fever had been wiped out completely. And malaria, another deadly disease, had been greatly reduced.

Oil is sprayed on a swamp near a military camp to kill mosquito larvae.

A Better Plan

Congress decided that a canal with **locks** would be cheaper and faster to build than a sea-level canal. The plan called for building the Gatun Dam to hold back the water of the Chagres River. This created a huge lake that ships could navigate. Locks at both ends of the canal would raise or lower the ships into the water as needed. This left an eight-mile stretch of land that had to be dug out to finish the canal connection from ocean to ocean.

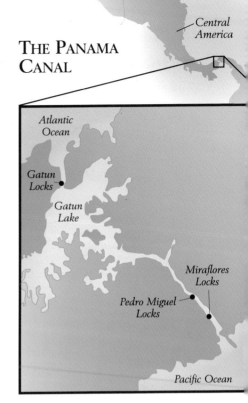

THE PANAMA CANAL

Central America

Atlantic Ocean

Gatun Locks

Gatun Lake

Miraflores Locks

Pedro Miguel Locks

Pacific Ocean

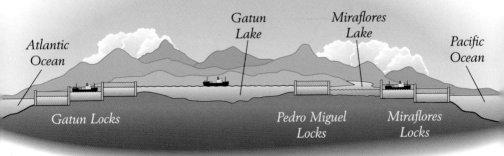

SIDE VIEW OF THE PANAMA CANAL

Gatun Lake

Miraflores Lake

Atlantic Ocean

Pacific Ocean

Gatun Locks

Pedro Miguel Locks

Miraflores Locks

Here is a view of the elevation changes in the Panama Canal. Locks allow ships to be raised or lowered to continue their passage through the canal.

Workers dig earth and rock by hand to reopen a stretch of the canal after a landslide during the canal's construction.

A Dangerous Dig

Digging an eight-mile **cut**, or man-made channel, was the hardest job. The land was made of a soft material. So as soon as workers dug a hole, more rock and earth would slide down into it. Before they were finished, engineers had to remove more than twice as much earth and rock than they had planned. Even trains and machines were buried under landslides.

This is the third landslide this week!

Other workers were hurt or killed by falling rocks, moving trains, and accidental explosions. And temperatures at the bottom of the channel could reach 120 degrees! This caused many sicknesses among the workers.

The Canal Opens

On August 15, 1914, a ship called the *Ancon* made the first complete trip through the Panama Canal from the Atlantic Ocean to the Pacific Ocean.

Today, more than 12,000 ships go through the canal each year—that's more than 33 every day. Until 1999, the United States had several military bases there. Thousands of troops and tons of war materials were shipped through the canal during several wars, including World War II. The country of Panama now controls and manages the canal.

The canal slogan, "The Land Divided, the World United," became a reality when the *Ancon* made the first official trip through the canal.

The Gatun Locks allow water into chambers that slowly raise or lower a ship to the level of the Gatun Lake. Then the ship can travel through the Panama Canal.

WHAT A PROJECT!

Here are some interesting facts about the building of the Panama Canal.

 WORKERS At the busiest time of construction, in 1913, more than 43,000 workers were on the job!

LOAVES OF BREAD On average each year, bakers made about six million loaves of bread for the canal workers.

 TRAIN CARS If you put all the material dug out to create the canal on a train of flat cars—the train would be long enough to go around the world four times!

EQUIPMENT Some of the equipment used: 101 steam shovels, 369 locomotives, 6,163 railroad cars, and 553 drills.

The *USS Nevada* moves through the Panama Canal. Sailors crowd the deck for a barbecue, a tradition when passing through the canal.

The Kennedy Space Center

Imagine the force it takes to send a rocket hurtling into space. Five . . . four . . . three . . . two . . . one . . . blastoff!

Suddenly the air is filled with an ear-splitting explosion. Massive flames and gushing gas shoot from the bottom of the rocket. The force of these rushing gases is so great that it thrusts the rocket into outer space. This is how the first astronauts traveled into space in the 1960s. The rockets that carried them were huge. And the equipment used to carry out the launch was like nothing else ever built before.

Scientists knew large-scale space exploration projects like this needed a large-scale area in which they could be built. So, the north end of a marshy island along the east coast of Florida—Merrit Island—became space exploration's home.

A New Space Complex

Space experts responded to President John F. Kennedy's challenge to land a man on the moon before 1970. They began by building a huge complex at what is now called the Kennedy Space Center.

Launch Complex 39

On Merrit Island, work began on a **facility** called Launch Complex 39. This place was where the huge launch vehicles and spacecrafts of the Apollo mission would be built and launched. These missions would carry men to the moon and back.

At 9:32 AM on July 16, 1969, the manned space vehicle Apollo 11/Saturn V lifted off. This historic mission was the first to land men on the moon.

Launch Pad 39A

Launch Pad 39B

Vehicle Assembly
Building (VAB)

Locating near the ocean allows heavy pieces of rocket to arrive by barge. Launching over water is safer in case of crashes.

Launch Complex 39 became a collection of buildings, runways, platforms, and launch towers. Structures had to be massive enough to accommodate the machinery, launch pads, and roadways needed to fit the Saturn V launch vehicle and the Apollo spacecraft. Years later, the space shuttle would be moved on the same roadways.

Walking on the moon during the Apollo 11 mission

Vehicle Assembly Building

One of the most impressive buildings of Launch Complex 39 was the Vehicle Assembly Building (VAB)—one of the world's largest buildings. It had to be tall because the Apollo 15/Saturn V spacecraft was 100 feet taller than the Statue of Liberty. And that spacecraft had to be able to stand upright inside the VAB. Because of its height, engineers worried that the VAB would not be able to stand up to strong winds, including hurricanes. So, they built it on more than 4,000 steel pipes. These pipes were driven more than 160 feet underground into solid rock!

The Apollo 15/Saturn V space vehicle leaves the VAB.

Vehicle Assembly Building (VAB) under construction in January, 1965.

The transporter carries the 12.8-million pound Apollo 12/Saturn V space vehicle from the VAB in 1969.

Getting the Rocket Ready

The Apollo team worked on the Saturn V rocket inside the Vehicle Assembly Building. The rocket sat on top of a platform that had four hold-down arms, hook-like arms that kept the rocket in place. A huge tower that carried electrical power, fuel, and fluids to the rocket stood on the platform next to the rocket. And on top of the tower was a large crane that could lift up the heavy rocket pieces.

This interior view of the Apollo 11 Lunar Module shows Astronaut Edwin E. Aldrin, Jr., lunar module pilot, during the first lunar landing mission.

It's Launch Time!

Once the rocket is ready, how does it get out of the Vehicle Assembly Building and onto the launch pad?

Crawling to the Launch Pad

A massive **crawler**, with a platform larger than a baseball diamond, slowly moves along on tracks toward the rocket in the VAB. It fits under the rocket platform and lifts up the huge space vehicle onto the crawler. The crawler is designed to keep the rocket perfectly level as it slowly transports it to the launch pad three and a half miles away.

Today Launch Complex 39, which was designed for the Apollo program, has been modified for space shuttle operations.

HOW BIG AND HOW SLOW?

The crawler vehicle that moved the Apollo/SaturnV spacecraft from the VAB to the launch pad is the largest ground vehicle ever built. It weighs six million pounds and can carry twelve million pounds of spacecraft. It can only travel at one mile per hour with the spacecraft on it, so the 3.5-mile trip to the launch pad takes over three hours!

I thought that I was slow!

Blasting off, the manned Gemini spacecraft sits atop a Titan launch vehicle. During this four-day mission, astronaut Ed White completed the first American spacewalk.

Blast Off

At the launch pad, the rocket is prepared for launch. When it's ready for take-off, the engines are started. Fire and smoke fill the air. The four hold-down arms fall away. The rocket is released, and it shoots into the sky.

And we still wonder:
How did they do that?

Fact File

Experts have found signs that indicate some of the pyramid laborers may have been women!

On Merrit Island—before they were sprayed—as many as 500 mosquitoes would land on a person in a minute!

The fare for going through the Panama Canal is based on weight. The lowest fare was 36 cents, paid by a man who swam through the canal!

Each side of a steel canal gate weighs 700 tons. And the locks themselves have never had to be replaced!

Glossary

astronomer a scientist who studies the stars and planets

crawler a vehicle that travels slowly on chain belts

cut a man-made channel dug out of the land

facility something that is built for a particular purpose

isthmus a narrow strip of land that links two larger areas of land and has water on both sides

landslides rocks and earth sliding down slopes

locks enclosed spaces along a canal with watertight gates at each end that are used to raise and lower ships

mummified dried out and preserved after death in the manner of the ancient Egyptians

peasants people who usually work as laborers for landowners

pharaoh an ancient Egyptian king who the Egyptians believed was part god

sledges sleds on which heavy loads are dragged

pharaoh

Index